Medieval

Society

Kay Eastwood

Crabtree Publishing Company

www.crabtreebooks.com

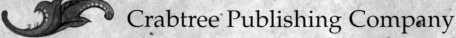

Crabtree Publishing Company

www.crabtreebooks.com

PMB 16A, 350 Fifth Avenue
Suite 3308
New York, NY 10118

612 Welland Avenue
St. Catharines
Ontario, Canada
L2M 5V6

73 Lime Walk
Headington
Oxford 0X3 7AD
United Kingdom

Coordinating editor: Ellen Rodger

Series editor: Carrie Gleason

Designer and production coordinator: Rosie Gowsell

Scanning technician: Arlene Arch-Wilson

Art director: Rob MacGregor

Project development, editing, photo editing, and layout:
First Folio Resource Group, Inc.: Erinn Banting, Tom Dart,
Jaimie Nathan, Debbie Smith, Anikó Szocs

Photo research: Maria DeCambra

Prepress: Embassy Graphics

Printing: Worzalla Publishing Company

Consultants: Joseph Goering, Department of History, University
of Toronto; Linda Northrup, Department of Near and Middle
Eastern Civilizations, University of Toronto; David Waterhouse,
Professor Emeritus of East Asian Studies, University of Toronto

Photographs: Archivo Iconografico, S.A./Corbis/
magmaphoto.com: p. 4, p. 6, p. 10 (bottom), p. 15 (top), p. 24; Art
Archive/British Library: p. 14, p. 17 (bottom); Art Archive/Musée
Calvet Avignon/Dagli Orti: p. 25 (top); Art Archive/Musée
Thomas Dobrée Nantes/Dagli Orti: p. 12 (bottom); Art
Archive/Topkapi Museum Istanbul/Dagli Orti: p. 28, p. 29 (top);
Art Archive/University Library Heidelberg/Dagli Orti: title page,
p. 13 (bottom); Art Archive/Victoria and Albert Museum
London/Graham Brandon: p. 16; Bettman/Corbis/
magmaphoto.com: p. 5; Bibliothèque Nationale, France/Arabe
5847 fol. 5v: p. 29; British Library/Bridgeman Art Library: p. 15
(bottom); British Library/Harley 4431, f. 144: p. 11 (bottom left);
Burstein Collection/Corbis/magmaphoto.com:
p. 31 (bottom); Christie's Images/Corbis/magmaphoto.com:
p. 23 (top); Elio Ciol/Corbis/magmaphoto.com: p. 25 (bottom);
Mary Evans Picture Library: p. 8 (bottom), p. 9; Giraudon/Art
Resource, NY: p. 13 (top); Historical Picture Archive/Corbis/
magmaphoto.com: p. 20; Erich Lessing/Art Resource, NY: p. 12
(top); North Wind Picture Archives: p. 22; Gianni Dagli
Orti/Corbis/magmaphoto.com: p. 21 (all); Pierpont Morgan
Library, MS. M.399, fol. 5v/Art Resource, NY: p. 17 (top); Réunion
des Musées Nationeaux/Art Resource, NY: p. 10 (top); Sakamoto
Photo Research Laboratory/Corbis/magmaphoto.com: p. 30;
Scala/Art Resource, NY: cover, p. 8 (top), p. 26 (top right); Heini
Schneebeli/Bridgeman Art Library: p. 31 (top); Snark/Art
Resource, NY: p. 7

Illustrations: Jeff Crosby: pp. 18-19; Katherine Kantor: flags, title
page (border), copyright page (bottom), p. 27 (middle, right);
Margaret Amy Reiach: borders, gold boxes, title page (illuminated
letter), copyright page (top), contents page (all), pp. 4--5
(timeline), p. 5 (map), p. 7 (top), p. 11 (top), p. 23 (bottom), p. 26
(middle and bottom), p. 27 (all), p. 29 (map), p. 32 (all)

Cover: Nobles return to the castle after a hunt. In the Middle
Ages, both noblemen and noblewomen hunted for sport and for
fresh meat to serve at their meals.

Title page: Minstrels, or musicians, play drums, fiddles, and other
instruments at a noble's feast. In return, the minstrels receive food
and a place to stay.

Published by
Crabtree Publishing Company

Copyright © 2004

Cataloging-in-Publication Data
Eastwood, Kay.
    Medieval society / written by Kay Eastwood.
        p. cm. -- (Medieval world series)
Summary: Describes daily life in Europe during the Middle Ages, looking at the
social hierarchy of the feudal system, through which kings and lords became rich
while peasants remained poor.
Includes bibliographical references and index.
    ISBN 0-7787-1345-8 (RLB) -- ISBN 0-7787-1377-6 (pbk)
1. Civilization, Medieval--Juvenile literature. 2. Europe--Social life and customs--
Juvenile literature. 3. Kings and rulers, Medieval--Juvenile literature. 4. Middle
Ages--Juvenile literature. 5. Cities and towns, Medieval--Europe--Juvenile
literature. [1. Civilization, Medieval. 2. Europe--Social life and customs. 3. Kings,
queens, rulers, etc. 4. Feudalism. 5. Middle Ages. 6. Cities and towns, Medieval.]
I. Title. II. Series.
    D117.E27 2004
    940.1--dc22   2003018227
                                                         LC

Table of Contents

The Middle Ages

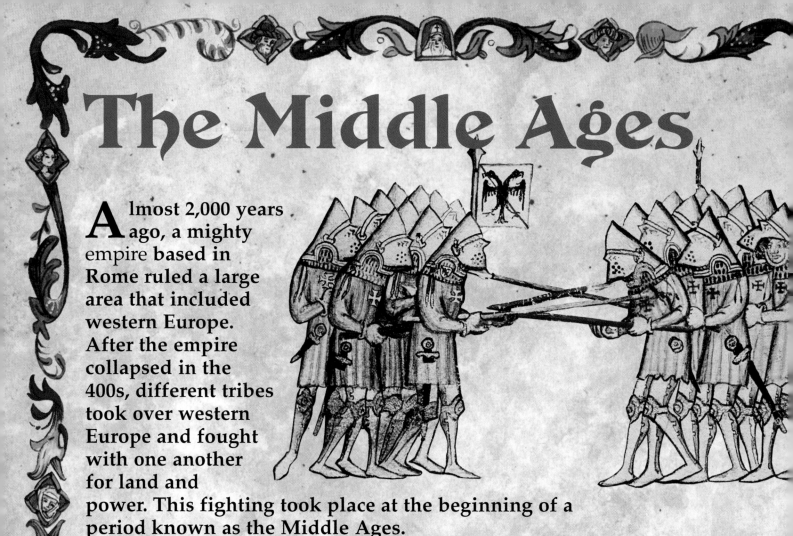

Almost 2,000 years ago, a mighty empire **based in Rome** ruled a large area that included western Europe. After the empire collapsed in the 400s, different tribes took over western Europe and fought with one another for land and **power. This fighting took place at the beginning of a period known as the Middle Ages.**

The Middle Ages lasted from 500 A.D. to 1500 A.D. During this time, countries formed and were ruled by kings. Kings tried to protect their subjects, or the people on their lands, from the attacks of Vikings from the north, Magyars from the east, and **Muslims** from the south. Within Europe, kings and lords, who were also part of the ruling class, or nobility, battled each other for land and power. At times, **peasants** also fought nobles to try to improve their lives.

▲ *Warriors in the 1300s often wore helmets with visors protecting their eyes, nose, and mouth. The warriors could open the visors to see and breathe better.*

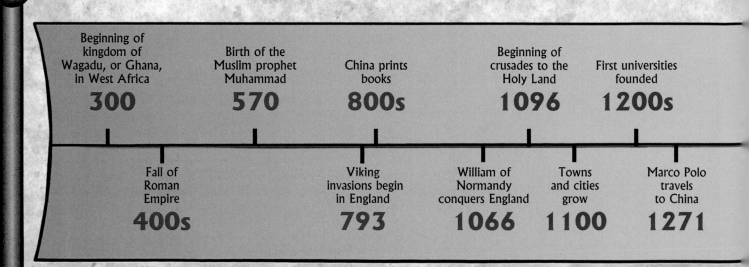

Beginning of kingdom of Wagadu, or Ghana, in West Africa	Birth of the Muslim prophet Muhammad	China prints books	Beginning of crusades to the Holy Land	First universities founded
300	**570**	**800s**	**1096**	**1200s**
Fall of Roman Empire	Viking invasions begin in England	William of Normandy conquers England	Towns and cities grow	Marco Polo travels to China
400s	**793**	**1066**	**1100**	**1271**

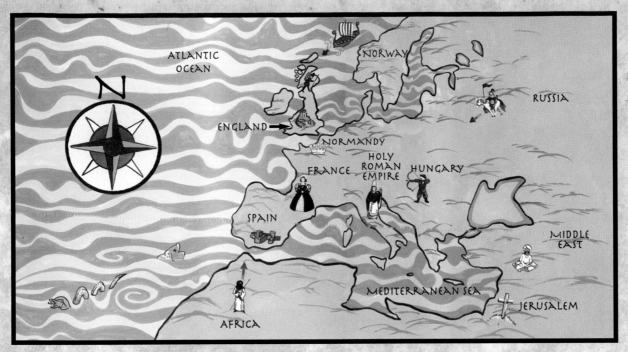

▲ *People from western Europe who fought in faraway lands during the Middle Ages brought new foods, jewels, and ideas about education back to Europe with them.*

Trade

The Middle Ages was also a time of **trade** with other countries. Merchants in Europe bought goods such as gold, silk, and spices from China, India, Africa, and the Middle East. They sold these goods at fairs in growing European cities. Artists created beautiful paintings and sculptures, the first universities were founded, and the introduction of the printing press made books cheaper to make and buy, so more people learned how to read.

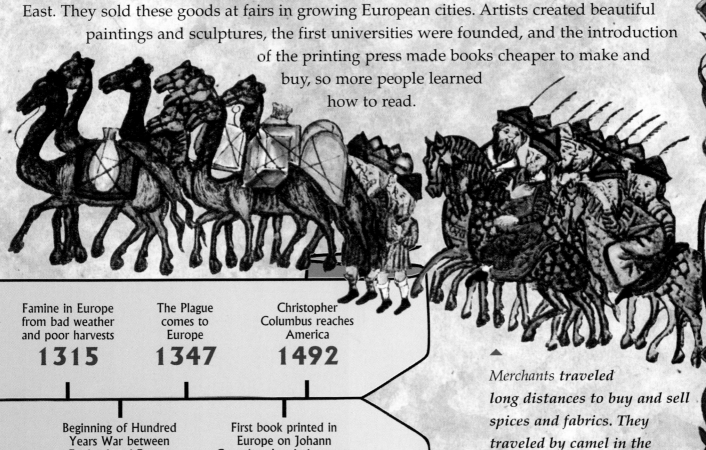

Famine in Europe from bad weather and poor harvests	The Plague comes to Europe	Christopher Columbus reaches America
1315	**1347**	**1492**

Beginning of Hundred Years War between England and France	First book printed in Europe on Johann Gutenberg's printing press
1337	**1455**

▲ *Merchants traveled long distances to buy and sell spices and fabrics. They traveled by camel in the deserts of the Middle East.*

Feudal Society

In the Middle Ages, the most powerful people in western Europe were great nobles, such as kings and lords, who controlled large areas of land. To protect their territories from other nobles and from outside invaders, they gave smaller areas of land, called fiefs, to their loyal supporters.

In exchange, the supporters, who were less important nobles, promised to become the **vassals** of their **overlords**. They had to obey their overlords at all times, fight for them during wars, and provide them with additional warriors, called knights.

The vassals paid the knights by giving them parts of their fiefs, called manors. The knights lived on the manors and collected rents from peasants who farmed the land. In return, the knights fought for the vassals for 40 days a year. Over time, knights became nobles too.

Peasants farmed the land of the manor in return for protection from invaders and small plots of land on which to grow their own crops and build small homes. This system of exchanging land for military service and other types of work is called feudalism, or the feudal system.

▲ *The promise vassals made to their overlords was called an oath of fealty, and they swore this oath on their knees. Even great lords had to swear an oath to their overlord, the king.*

End of Feudalism

Feudalism started to disappear in the 1200s because nobles fought fewer battles with one another and did not need armies of knights as they once did. By the 1300s, kings had complete control of their countries and nobles had little power. Kings still fought wars with other countries, but they hired soldiers, called mercenaries, to fight for them. The mercenaries fought for as long as they were paid, not just the 40 days a year that knights fought.

The feudal structure looks like a pyramid. The most powerful people in society, the kings and a few great lords, were at the top of the pyramid. Most people in society were peasants, at the bottom of the pyramid. They had the least power.

◀ King

◀ Great lords

◀ Lesser nobles

◀ Knights

◀ Peasants

▼ *Peasants plowed fields with the help of oxen. Peasants wore clothes that women made from wool or coarse linen. Men wore short belted tunics and stockings, and women wore long dresses and kerchiefs on their heads.*

Kings and Queens

Kings ruled over large territories called kingdoms. It was the king's duty to create laws for his kingdom, defend his people from outside enemies, and keep peace among the nobles who lived on his land. Some kings, especially in the early Middle Ages, did not have much power over their nobles. The nobles were sometimes wealthier than the king.

Becoming a King

A king was crowned in an extravagant ceremony called a coronation. The pope, who was the head of the **Christian** Church, or another important Church leader placed the crown on the king's head. This ceremony showed the people that the king was chosen by God, and that it was the king's duty to protect the Christian Church.

Queens

Queens, who were married to kings, came from very powerful families and were daughters of other kings or great lords. A queen often owned a large area of land, which she brought with her to her marriage. This made the size of her husband's kingdom even larger, and it made the king even more powerful. Queens offered their husbands advice on how to rule the kingdom. When a king was away fighting a war, his queen was often left in charge.

◀ *Eleanor of Aquitaine (1122–1204) was one of the most powerful women of the Middle Ages. She ruled her own territories in Aquitaine, which is an area in modern-day France, and married the kings of both France and England.*

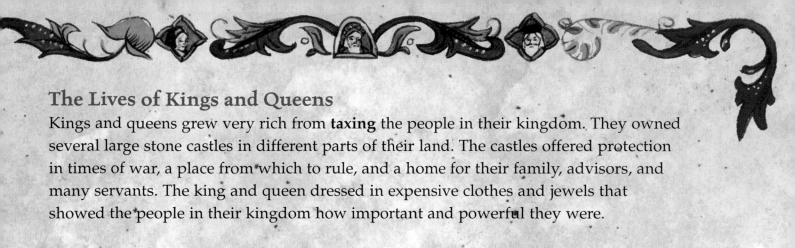

The Lives of Kings and Queens

Kings and queens grew very rich from **taxing** the people in their kingdom. They owned several large stone castles in different parts of their land. The castles offered protection in times of war, a place from which to rule, and a home for their family, advisors, and many servants. The king and queen dressed in expensive clothes and jewels that showed the people in their kingdom how important and powerful they were.

Troubles with Nobles

Kings had a great deal of power, but they still had to treat their subjects fairly if they wanted their kingdom to run smoothly. In 1215, the nobles of England rebelled against King John I, who had raised their taxes and taken away some of their power.

On June 15, the nobles forced the king to sign a document called the *Magna Carta*, or "Great Charter," which stated that the king was not all powerful. He was not allowed to pass laws without consulting his people; he had to follow laws just like everyone else; and he could not arrest or imprison anyone without a fair trial. These ideas later became important rules for the way England and the U.S. are governed.

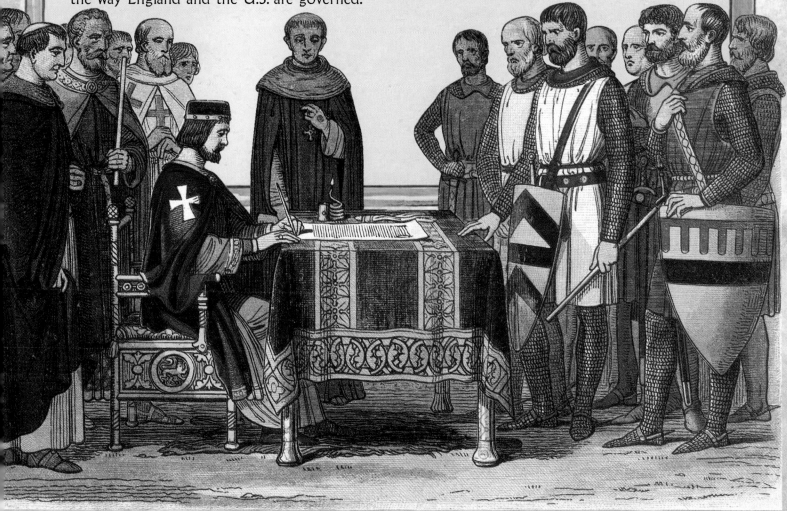

Lords

A lord looked after his manor from his castle or manor home. He protected the people who lived on his manor, collected taxes from them, and punished those who broke the law. The lord controlled everything on the manor, including the mills and bread ovens, where peasants paid to grind their grain and bake their bread.

▲ Lords had many servants in their castles, including some who took care of the hawks and falcons used to hunt small birds and rabbits.

◀ Lords liked to show off their wealth by eating well. Many fancy dishes were served at their great feasts. After the meal, musicians, dancers, acrobats, and jugglers performed for the lord and his guests.

Looking After the Manor

Some lords had manors in different parts of the country. Stewards or bailiffs looked after each manor for the lord. The lord visited from time to time to make sure there were no problems.

When the lord was not fighting for his overlord or taking care of his manor, he hunted wild animals and played games such as chess and backgammon. He also held large feasts to celebrate the births of his children, their marriages, visits from important people, and religious festivals.

▲ *Lords hunted deer, boars, bears, and wolves for fun and for exercise. Hunting was also good training for war.*

Silk and Finery

Lords could afford fine fabrics, such as silk, for their clothing. All their clothes were measured and made for them by tailors.

By the 1300s, to make sure that wealthy merchants were not confused with nobles, and craftspeople were not confused with wealthy merchants, laws were passed in towns about what kind of clothes each group could wear. For example, only the most powerful nobles were allowed to dress in purple silk or in gold or silver cloth.

Ladies

A noblewoman was called a lady. A lady usually married a nobleman her parents chose for her. Noble marriages were arranged to increase the wealth, land, and power of both families. It did not matter if the nobleman and noblewoman loved each other.

In the Middle Ages, the most important responsibility of a lady was to have sons to carry on the family name and **inherit** the family land. A healthy noblewoman often had a baby every year from the age of fourteen until she was in her mid-30s. Many of these children died young from illnesses and accidents.

▼ *Weddings were first held in churches in the mid 1100s. Here, a* bishop *marries a king and a noblewoman.*

▲ *Noblewomen wore elaborate dresses and hats to show off their wealth.*

Running the Castle

A lady was also responsible for running a large, busy household. She planned meals, ordered supplies from the nearest village or town, and supervised the servants. When her husband was away fighting or visiting his other manors, she defended the manor if it was attacked and took care of any manor business. In her spare time, she **embroidered**, played chess, read stories about knights, ladies, and love, and went hunting with her husband.

Ladies taught young girls from other noble families how to manage a household and behave like a lady. These girls, sometimes called ladies-in-waiting, came to live in the lady's home when they were seven or eight years old.

▲ *Noblewomen gave birth in the castle, with the help of their friends and maidservants.*

▼ *Lords and ladies enjoyed playing chess. European travelers learned chess from the Muslims they met when overseas. It was a game of strategy and war that involved nobles just like the lords and ladies.*

Knights

During the Middle Ages, knights who fought on horseback were the most important warriors on the battlefield. Their horses allowed them to charge at the enemy with great speed and force.

Knights fought for their overlords against other lords. They also fought in holy wars called crusades. During the crusades, Christian knights from Europe traveled to the Middle East. There, they fought Muslims for control of the Holy Land, the area where Jesus Christ was born, lived, and died.

Tournaments

When knights were not fighting, they practiced their skills at competitions called tournaments. Tournaments included melees, which were battles between two groups of warriors, and jousting contests. The goal of a joust was for one knight to knock his opponent off his horse by charging at him with a long pole called a lance.

▲ *Everyone, from kings to peasants, gathered to watch tournaments. Nobles watched from elevated boxes, while everyone else watched from the sides.*

Pages and Squires

A noble boy began training to be a knight when he was about seven years old. He went to live at the home of another lord where, at first, he worked as a page. He ran errands and served meals to the lord. He learned good manners, how to ride a horse, and how to use small weapons.

When the page was around fourteen years old, he became a squire to a knight. He carried his knight's shield, looked after his horses, helped him put on his armor, and learned how to use full-sized weapons.

A squire was dubbed a knight when he was 21, or earlier if he was especially brave. The dubbing ceremony was one of the most important events of a young man's life.

At the dubbing ceremony, the squire knelt before his overlord, who tapped his shoulder gently with the flat part of his sword. Afterward, the new knight was given his own sword. Squires from very important families were sometimes dubbed by the king himself.

Chivalry

Knights followed a code of honor called chivalry. A chivalrous knight was brave, loyal, generous, polite, and honest. He protected the weak, including widows and children, and defended the Christian religion. He also promised to treat ladies with respect, and often fought tournaments to impress the woman he loved.

▶ *The Church established the rules of chivalry because knights were not always well-behaved. When they were not fighting, many early knights terrorized the local people, which included stealing their food.*

Peasants

Most people in the Middle Ages were peasants who lived in small villages on their lord's manor. For two or three days each week, they farmed the lord's land, looked after his livestock, and did other work for him, such as repairing buildings on the manor.

The rest of the week, peasants worked on their own small pieces of land where they grew food for their families. Some peasants did not have land, only a house in the village and a small garden.

Farmland

The village was surrounded by three large fields. Peasants planted crops that grew in the winter, such as wheat and rye, in one field. They planted crops that grew in the spring and summer, such as peas, lentils, beans, barley, and oats, in a second field. Each year, they left one field fallow, which means that they did not plant any crops there so that the land could regain its **nutrients**. Each field was divided into long, narrow strips. Peasants received several strips in each field so that everyone shared the good and poor land.

▼ *In late summer, peasants worked together to bring in the harvest. They cut wheat with scythes, and gathered it into bundles which they stored in the village.*

Peasants' Homes

Peasant families usually lived together in one or two rooms, in small homes built from stone or wattle and daub. Wattle was a frame of wood and woven twigs. It was filled with daub, a mixture of mud, straw, and animal dung. The roofs of most peasant homes were thatched with a thick layer of straw, reeds, and other plants such as heather. To brighten the walls and protect them from rain, peasants painted their homes with a white substance called lime.

There were very few items in a peasant's home, usually just a table, a bench, a storage chest, and a few tools for cooking and farming. There was no running water or indoor plumbing. Water was brought from the village well, and the toilet was a pit in the yard.

▲ *Peasant women were in charge of milking the cows and making butter and cheese. In the winter, shepherds kept their sheep and goats in the village where they could take care of them more easily.*

Food and Drink

Peasants ate very simple meals of dark, heavy bread, cooked vegetables and fruit, and occasionally meat, eggs, or cheese. Pottage, or porridge, was made from boiled barley or oats with peas, onions, garlic, and bacon if it was available. A weak alcoholic drink made from grains called ale was the most common drink, even for children.

▶ *Peasants worked together to make sure there was enough food to eat.*

A Peasant's Year

Animals are put out to graze in the pasture.

Crops such as oats, barley, peas, and beans were planted.

Crops are weeded.

Women make cheese and butter from cows' and sheep's milk.

Sheep are sheared.

Spring

Summer

Spring and Summer

A peasant's life changed depending on the season. In the spring, peasants planted their summer crops and let their animals graze in the pasture. In summer, peasants sheared the sheep and tended the crops by watering and weeding as they prayed for a bountiful harvest that autumn.

Autumn

Wheat planted the winter before is cut and bound.

Hay from the grass in the meadows is cut to feed the livestock over the winter.

Crops are harvested from the fields.

Livestock is fattened up for winter slaughter.

Doors are put on homes as the nights grow colder.

Winter

Winter crops of wheat and rye are planted.

Fields are plowed before the ground freezes.

When the temperature gets colder, peasants fix their tools, repair buildings, and rest.

Animals are brought in from the pasture.

Wood is collected for fuel.

Autumn and Winter

Autumn was harvest time, the busiest time of the year. Not only did peasants harvest their own crops, but they harvested their lord's crops too. Early winter was spent planting winter crops and slaughtering animals that peasants could not afford to feed over the next few months. The meat was preserved with salt so that it would not spoil before peasants ate it.

Townspeople

By the 1100s, new inventions, such as better plows, made it easier to farm. Peasants grew more crops than they needed to feed their families and to pay their lord. They began to hold weekly or monthly markets at crossroads to trade their products for goods from other manors.

Soon, craftspeople, such as weavers and goldsmiths, and food and beverage sellers moved to the areas around the markets and opened shops. These people earned money by making and selling goods rather than by farming or fighting.

▼ In the late Middle Ages, some cities had indoor markets where merchants sold goods of all kinds. Here, shoppers browse at a stall that has shoes and boots, and another with plates and other items for the table.

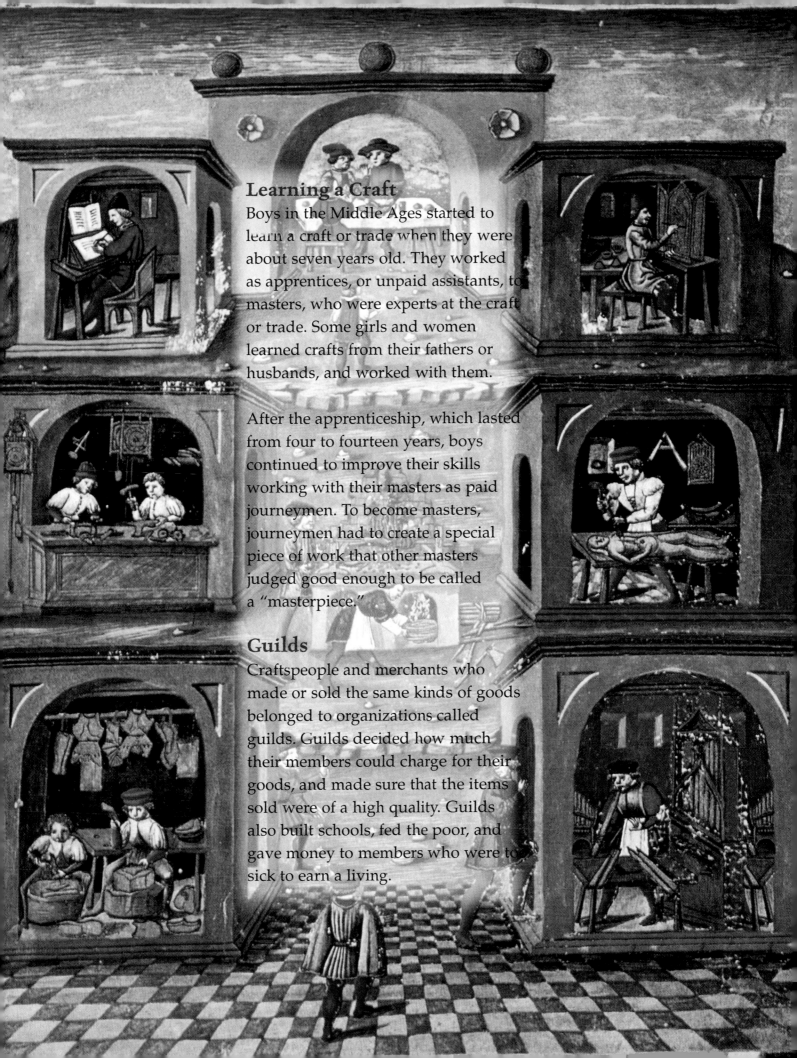

Learning a Craft

Boys in the Middle Ages started to learn a craft or trade when they were about seven years old. They worked as apprentices, or unpaid assistants, to masters, who were experts at the craft or trade. Some girls and women learned crafts from their fathers or husbands, and worked with them.

After the apprenticeship, which lasted from four to fourteen years, boys continued to improve their skills working with their masters as paid journeymen. To become masters, journeymen had to create a special piece of work that other masters judged good enough to be called a "masterpiece."

Guilds

Craftspeople and merchants who made or sold the same kinds of goods belonged to organizations called guilds. Guilds decided how much their members could charge for their goods, and made sure that the items sold were of a high quality. Guilds also built schools, fed the poor, and gave money to members who were too sick to earn a living.

Life in Towns

The most powerful people in towns were wealthy merchants. They traded goods such as cloth, fur, and wood for silk, spices, and perfumes from Asia, jewels from Persia and India, and salt, gold, and ivory from Africa. There were also many craftspeople, shop owners, and merchants who traded goods bought locally.

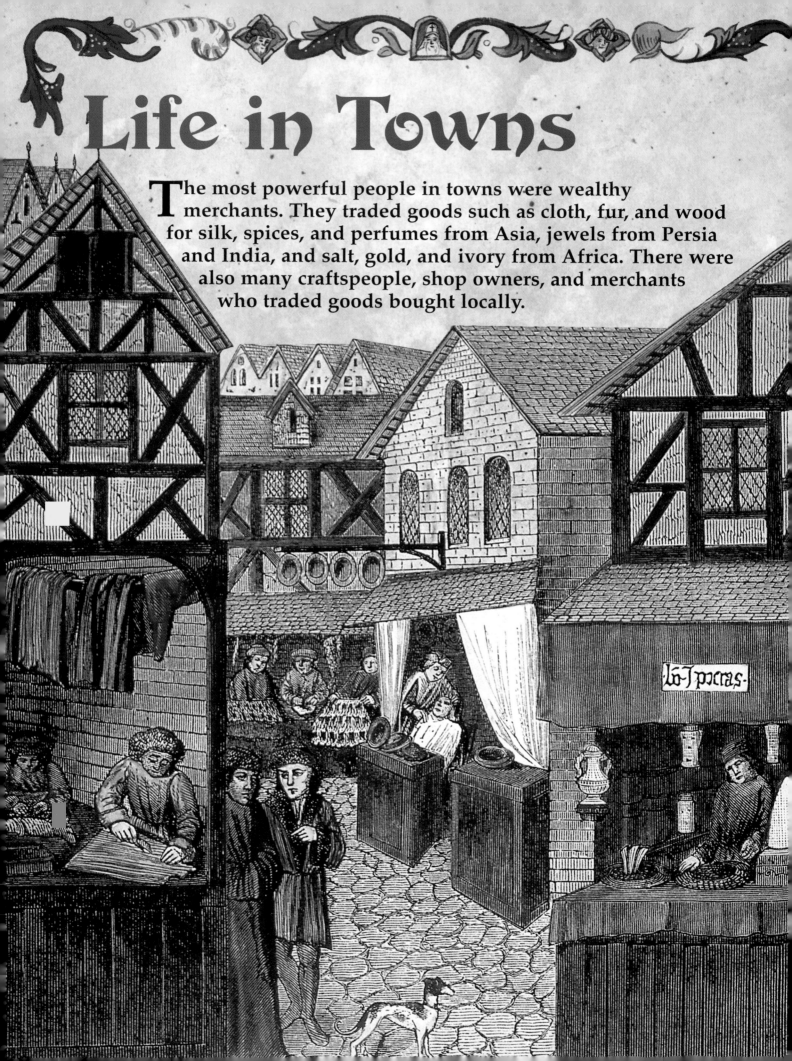

Servants

Most people in towns and cities were servants. They worked for all but the poorest families, cooking, cleaning, and helping in businesses. Some people could not find a job or a place to live. They had to sleep on the streets and survive by begging.

Town Homes

People in towns lived in narrow houses that were three or four stories high. On the ground floor was a workshop where a craftsperson worked, or a shop and storeroom where a merchant sold and stored his goods. The second floor had a kitchen, a room where the family ate, and the husband and wife's bedroom. The children and servants slept in the attic on the top floor. In the back were stables, storehouses, and an outhouse, where people went to the bathroom. People also kept chamber pots in their bedrooms so that they did not have to go to the outhouse in the middle of the night.

▲ *After a day's work, servants gathered outside taverns to drink ale and eat a meal.*

Sanitation

The most common way to get rid of garbage, such as spoiled vegetables, sawdust from carpenters' shops, and human and animal waste, was to dump it into the streets. Medieval townspeople were always careful not to step into something unpleasant or get hit by the contents of a chamber pot thrown from an upper story.

Street sweepers worked at night, sweeping all the waste into an open sewer that ran down the center of the street. A stream carried this waste outside the city into the surrounding fields or into a river. Some cities hired people to cart the garbage outside the city. Medieval cities smelled terrible, especially during the hot summer months.

By the 1300s, most European towns and cities had public bathhouses where people bathed. Some bathhouses were large enough to have separate areas for men and women.

Religion

In the Middle Ages, Christianity was the main religion in Europe. Christians believe in one God and follow the teachings of his son on earth, Jesus Christ. There are many denominations, or kinds, of Christianity today, but in the Middle Ages, Roman Catholicism was the only denomination in western Europe.

Religion played an important part in medieval people's lives. Christians were supposed to go to church every Sunday, confess their **sins** to their **priest**, and not eat meat three days a week. They also had to give one tenth of their income, called the tithe, to the Church.

The Local Church

The church was the most important building in the community. Local people gathered there to hear **Mass** on Sundays and to celebrate **baptisms** and marriages. They met outside the church to talk about village business or to chat with friends. If the community had a school, it was usually in the church.

▲ *Large churches had windows with beautiful panes of stained glass. The windows told stories from the Bible, the Christian holy book. This was one way that people who did not know how to read could learn the Bible.*

24

◀ Saints

Many churches were built to honor saints. Saints are holy people who Catholics believe can ask God to perform miracles, such as curing the sick, making crops grow, and protecting people from danger.

Some people in the Middle Ages traveled great distances on religious journeys, called pilgrimages, to visit the place where a saint was buried or where objects belonging to a saint were kept. These objects, called relics, were sometimes pieces of the saint's body, such as a tooth or finger.

In the Middle Ages, each village, town, and city had a saint who protected the community. A special holiday was held on the anniversary of the saint's birth or death. Everyone went to church for Mass. Afterward, a statue of the saint was carried through the streets so that people could pay their respects. The rest of the day was spent singing, dancing, and feasting.

Cradle to Grave

Special church ceremonies marked each stage of a person's life. A baptism welcomed a baby into the Church. In a confirmation, older children became full members of the Church. Couples married in or at the doors of churches, with God, their families, and friends as witnesses. When people were about to die, the priest heard their last confession. Then, they were buried inside the church or at a cemetery near the church, on ground that was considered holy.

Devoted to God

Many Christians in the Middle Ages devoted their lives to God. They preached the word of God, led Christian ceremonies, studied the Bible, and helped poor and sick people in the community.

◀ The Pope

The pope is the leader of the Roman Catholic Church. In the Middle Ages, the pope was very powerful because Catholics believed he was God's representative on earth. The pope controlled kings by threatening to excommunicate them, or ban them from the Church, if they did not do as he asked. If the king still did not listen, the pope put the king's kingdom under interdict. This meant that no one in the kingdom was allowed to go to church or hear Mass.

Bishops ▶

The pope chose a bishop to look after the religious needs of the people in a large area called a diocese. Bishops were well educated and often became very rich and powerful because they advised kings, from whom they received land. They also received land from nobles who hoped that their gifts would help them get into heaven. Many bishops were younger sons from noble families who chose the Church as a good way to earn a living.

◀ Priests

Priests led prayer services in local churches and performed ceremonies such as weddings and baptisms. Priests in small villages often had very little education. Many could not read their Bibles, which were written in Latin, the language of educated people. Instead, the priests memorized prayers and important parts of the Bible to teach the people in their church.

Monks ▶

Monks were men who devoted their lives to prayer and study. They lived in special communities called monasteries that were in the countryside. A monastery was like a manor built around a large church, with its own workshops, farms, gardens, orchards, barns, and land. Monks had to follow certain rules. They were not allowed to own any personal possessions or have any contact with women. Some were not even allowed to speak except to pray.

◀ Nuns

Nuns were unmarried women who spent their lives praying, studying, and helping the sick. Their communities were called convents. Some girls became nuns instead of marrying a man that their families chose for them. Other girls entered convents so they could be taught by nuns, who were well educated.

Friars ▶

Friars were educated men who traveled between villages, towns, and cities preaching the word of God and doing good deeds. They gave up all their money and possessions, and lived by begging.

Muslim Society

During the Middle Ages, a religion called Islam spread to many parts of the world. The people who follow Islam are called Muslims. Muslims believe in one God, Allah, and in the teachings of his prophets, especially Muhammad.

As Muslims spread their religion, they created a great trading empire. Merchants from all over the Muslim world met in enormous **bazaars** in cities such as Baghdad, in present-day Iraq, to sell silks, spices, and horses from China, silver and cotton from India, and gold and ivory from Africa.

◀ *Sultans, who led Muslim states, had many servants to wait on them and musicians to entertain them.*

Education was very important to medieval Muslims, who translated ancient Greek writings into Arabic, the language of the **Qur'an**. Muslims were much more advanced in areas such as medicine and astronomy than most people in western Europe.

Muslim Cities

Cities in Muslim lands were filled with **mosques**, hospitals, libraries, and colleges where students learned Muslim law and studied the writings of ancient Greek **philosophers** and doctors. Scientists invented instruments such as astrolabes and sundials to study planets and other objects in the sky. Craftspeople created beautiful tiles and rugs that were covered in geometric designs, flowers, and writings from the *Qur'an*, the Muslim holy book. Important works of literature, including *The Thousand and One Nights*, a collection of fairy tales, fables, legends, adventure stories, and poems, were published.

After Allah began revealing his teachings to Muhammad in 610 A.D., Muhammad and his followers spread the new religion of Islam through the Middle East, Africa, Spain, India, and Southeast Asia.

EUROPE

ASIA
750s

SPAIN
711

MIDDLE
EAST

AFRICA
710

JERUSALEM
637

IRAN
651

EGYPT
644

INDIA
1200s

MECCA
622

Medieval World

There were great cultures outside Muslim and Christian lands in the Middle Ages. Each culture had its own type of ruler and its own way of life.

Imperial Japan

Medieval Japan was ruled by an emperor, but starting around 1150, strong military leaders held the real power. These leaders were called *shoguns*.

The *shogun* allowed his most trusted vassals to control large estates. In return, the vassals promised to be loyal and to give the *shogun* a share of the taxes they collected from the peasants who farmed the land. The vassals loaned parts of their estates to less important families, who agreed to fight for them. The warriors were called samurai. Over time, they became nobles, like European knights.

By the 1400s, the *shogun* lost all of his power to local military leaders, called *daimyo*, who fought one another for control of the countryside. The *daimyo* gathered samurai warriors around their castle headquarters to protect them against rival *daimyo*.

▲ *Samurai warriors fought on horseback, like knights. Their armor was made from richly decorated plates of leather or iron that were laced together with brightly colored silk. This beautiful armor was supposed to inspire the samurai to do great and heroic deeds in battle.*

West Africa

The kingdom of Wagadu (300–1100) was in West Africa, south of the Sahara Desert. Its ruler was called "the Ghana." This is the name that people outside the kingdom gave the kingdom itself. The Ghana was in charge of the army and ruled with the help of a People's Council, whose members represented the people of the kingdom.

Wagadu became wealthy by collecting taxes from merchants who passed through the kingdom on their way to the Middle East with gold, salt, copper, and slaves. Most people of Wagadu farmed and made crafts, including pottery, cloth, and gold jewelry. Skilled ironworkers made iron-tipped spears that warriors used to conquer other African kingdoms. In the 1100s, the kingdom of Mali took over Wagadu, and the area became even wealthier and more powerful from trade.

▲ *To honor kings in Wagadu who died, artists sculpted clay heads that looked like the kings. Kings were buried with their possessions so they could use them in the afterlife, or life after death.*

Imperial China

During the Middle Ages, China was ruled by an emperor. When the emperor died, his eldest son became the new emperor. If an emperor was weak, a new family took over. Each family was called a dynasty.

By around 1000, the emperor ruled with the help of highly educated men who had to pass a very difficult examination. Many of these government officials came from successful families that made their living as craftspeople, poets, shopkeepers, merchants, and traders in China's growing cities. Most people in China were peasants who lived in the countryside and farmed the large estates of wealthy landowners. These landowners were often government officials.

▲ *Skilled Chinese silkweavers wove beautiful fabrics that were used to make clothing.*

Glossary

astronomy The study of the stars and planets

baptism A religious ceremony that welcomes a person to the Catholic Church

bazaar An area of small shops and stalls

bishop A high-ranking religious leader in the Catholic Church

Christian Belonging to the religion of Christianity, which follows the teachings of God and his son on earth, Jesus Christ

crossroads A central location where two or more roads meet

embroider To make a design in cloth using a needle and thread

empire A group of countries or territories under one ruler or government

inherit To receive money or possessions from someone who died

livestock Farm animals

Mass The main ceremony of the Roman Catholic Church

merchant A person who buys and sells goods

Middle East A region that is made up of southwestern Asia and northern Africa

mosque A sacred building in which Muslims pray

Muslim A person who believes in Islam, a religion based on the teachings of God, whom Muslims call Allah, and his prophet Muhammad

nutrient A substance that living things need in order to grow

overlord A lord who rules over other lords

peasant A person who owns or rents a small piece of land for farming

philosopher A person who tries to explain the laws of the universe

priest A person who leads religious ceremonies in the Catholic Church

prophet A person believed to carry God's message

sin A thought or action that goes against God's wishes

tavern A place where people drink alcohol

tax To request payment in the form of money, services, crops, or livestock

trade A type of business, usually one that involves working with the hands

vassal A person who promises loyalty to a lord in exchange for land and protection

Index

1 2 3 4 5 6 7 8 9 0   Printed in the U.S.A.   8 7 6 5 4 3

Kenmore Primary School

Kenmore Primary School